ACADEMIC EFFECTIVENESS:

A MANUAL FOR SCHOLASTIC SUCCESS

AT THE

UNITED STATES NAVAL ACADEMY

FOURTH EDITION

United States Naval Academy

Eric D. Bowman, Ph.D.

Director, Academic Center
United States Naval Academy

KENDALL/HUNT PUBLISHING COMPANY
4050 Westmark Drive   Dubuque, Iowa 52002

ACKNOWLEDGMENTS_____

I'd like to acknowledge the assistance I've received from Dr. Randy Smith, a Navy psychologist who first thought of placing all of the Academy's study skills materials into one packet. Several of the materials in this manual have been adapted from handouts the Naval Academy had been using.

I have also received very helpful suggestions from members of the Military Learning Assistance Board. This is a group of educational professionals at military institutions throughout the United States who have a common interest in providing learning skills assistance to their students. For the Third Edition, I have received added assistance from Gwendolyn Stevens, the Director of Academic Resources at the Coast Guard Academy in New London, CT. She has allowed me to use the article by Associate Professor Faye Ringle Hazel, Ph.D. The section on phrase reading in Chapter Four was adapted from material written by Mr. Lewis Fleischner of Learning Skills, Inc.

For the 1995 edition, I have received considerable assistance from several individuals. CDR Maureen Sullivan has contributed material about learning styles that she and Mr. Thomas Schulze have used in the Academic Effectiveness courses being taught at the Naval Academy. Ms. Debra M. Larson, and Mr. Robert Meehan, have provided invaluable assistance in the modifications to the chapter on time management. An additional change for this edition covering important information specific to studying Mathematics has been provided by Associate Professor Richard Maruszewski.

TABLE OF CONTENTS_____

Preface vii
Introduction for the Student ix

1 Getting Started 3
Academics at the Naval Academy 5
Personal Goals and Motivation 5
Learning Styles 8
Tips to Success at the Naval Academy 13

2 Time Management 15
Semester Calendar 17
Weekly Calendar 17
Daily Schedule 20

3 Classroom Note-Taking 31
Before the Lecture 32
During the Lecture 33
After the Lecture 34
Cornell Note-Taking System 36
Listening and Note-Taking Skills 38
How to Study Mathematics 39

4 Reading Effectiveness 45
Increasing Reading Speed 47
SQ3R Reading Method 50
Timed Reading Sample 53

5 Test Taking   **55**

Preparing for Exams   56
Objective Exams   58
Essay Exams   61

6 Stress Management   **67**

Stress and Breathing   71
Progressive Relaxation Exercise   73
Visualizations   74

7 Other USNA Resources   **79**

Academic Center   80
Chaplain Center   82
Chemistry Department Extra Instruction   82
Math Lab   82
Midshipmen Counseling   83
Writing Center   83

8 How To Avoid Plagiarism   **85**

Definition and History of the Concept of Plagiarism   86
Plagiarism and the Honor Concept   89
Research Papers and Other Written Assignments   90
Paraphrasing in Academic Writing   93
Methods of Documentation   97

Bibliography   103

PREFACE_____

When I first started teaching at the Naval Academy in 1984, I knew that all of the service academies actively recruited some of the best students that the United States has to offer. All candidates are highly screened for competitive appointments and must show high levels of leadership ability and academic success before they are selected for appointment.

At first glance, one would expect that every midshipman at the Naval Academy would have already learned all the basic skills necessary for success in an academic setting. They have, after all, already proven their academic ability by being among the top high school graduates in the country. It was a puzzle to me why there would be a need for study skills instruction. If these students are "the best and the brightest", why would any of them need instruction in the very basics of how to succeed in school? I soon discovered that most of the midshipmen with whom I was working *were* very bright. In fact, most were bright enough to have gotten very good grades in high school *without* efficient learning strategies. Midshipmen are bright enough and motivated enough to do quite well at almost any civilian college. However, the Naval Academy certainly is not a civilian college and life for the midshipmen is nothing like life on a civilian campus.

To begin with, most midshipmen take between 17 and 20 credit hours per semester. On top of that, all first year students (plebes) must learn what amounts to at least one full course of professional topics. Midshipmen are additionally required to spend three hours per day in athletic participation or drill. Being the "best and the brightest" is not enough. In order to succeed at the Naval Academy midshipmen must learn to be effective and efficient learners. That is what led to the creation of the Naval Academy's Academic Effectiveness Courses, and that is what eventually led to this manual.

As the title suggests, this manual is written specifically for use by mid-shipmen at the United States Naval Academy. Use by others is certainly not inappropriate. In fact, a modified form of this manual is being used by all Naval Reserve Officer Training Corps programs throughout the United States and an earlier edition was modified for use at the Coast Guard Academy. However, all examples that are used are directly applicable to Naval Academy life. It is the examples and application that make this manual unique.

There is an abundance of study skills manuals and text books available. I have listed some of the most valuable resources in the Bibliography. I have used several of them in the courses I have coordinated and taught at the Naval Academy, and, although the information they contain is valuable, all the materials have received unfavorable evaluations from midshipmen as well as instructors. The study skills materials that have been commercially available just do not apply to life at the Naval Academy. Any reference to scheduling for a part time student (there are no part-time students at the Academy), or suggestion that the average class load is 12–15 semester hours will elicit an immediate negative reaction. Thus it became clear to me that for any study skills material to be valuable to midshipmen, it had to be directly applicable to the Naval Academy, or at least applicable to life at any of the service academies.

This manual is designed to be used in two ways. First, it is being used as the main text for the Academic Effectiveness Courses that are available to Naval Academy midshipmen experiencing academic difficulty. All the basic study skills are covered. There are chapters on motivation (Getting Started), time management, note taking, reading, test taking, and stress management as well as a list of Academy resources. A bibliography has also been included for those students who wish to explore outside reading.

The second intended use of this manual is as a self-help reference. Although the skills necessary for academic success are all interrelated, it is possible to focus only on those skills relevant to a particular student. It is written so that students are able to select those areas upon which they wish to focus. It is my goal that this manual will be of value to all Naval Academy midshipmen who want to improve their academic effectiveness regardless of their specific academic standing.

INTRODUCTION FOR THE STUDENT_

The title says it all; **Academic Effectiveness: A Manual for Scholastic Success at the United States Naval Academy.** It is obvious who is the intended audience. This manual is designed specifically for you, a midshipman at the United States Naval Academy.

But why? Why does the Academy believe that you need any study skills instructions at all? Haven't you already proven your academic capabilities before you were even admitted? If you are reading this manual for the first time during your Plebe Summer, just wait! As most of you found out on I-Day, little of your previous experiences prepared you for what was to come. Likewise, your previous experiences with how to learn will only be of moderate help to you once the academic year begins.

You've been told, but don't really *know* yet, how important organizational skills will be. Efficiency is the key to effectiveness. Most of you will find there are not enough study hours available to allow you to obtain the grades you're used to. You must learn to be more efficient with the time you do have available. You can no longer waste time without suffering the consequences.

However, it is possible to train yourself to be an "attack student". You can begin right now to use the information in this manual to help yourself to success! If you are an upper class reading this manual for the first time, you know the truth of what I have already said. More than likely, you are reading this manual hoping to start fresh at the beginning of a new semester or possibly making a desperate attempt to salvage the present semester. In any case, the information in this manual is even more important to you. With hard work on your part you can save yourself. You too can remove yourself from the academic unsatisfactory list. The Superintendent's List is not out of the question!

But what makes this manual so special? With all the study skills materials available, why is this one different? I have attempted to use other manuals or text books in the study skills courses at the Academy. But midshipmen have consistently expressed concern that the materials developed for civilian students just didn't seem relevant. At first, I attributed this concern to resistance. I felt midshipmen just had to adapt; to be flexible. It was true that the examples were not exactly appropriate, but the underlying message was valuable. After all, students are students and learning is learning. It shouldn't make much difference whether we are talking about civilian or military students.

I was wrong. It does make a difference, and the difference is critical. If it is clear that an author is not talking about you, the value of the author's message is diminished for you. I wrote this manual in order to rectify the problems expressed by midshipmen and instructors who have participated in the Academic Effectiveness Courses at the Naval Academy.

Whether you are a plebe or an upper class, if you have been receiving high grades or low grades, the information in this manual can be helpful. Even the best students can fine tune their study skills. The fine tuning just might allow them a little extra free time. Almost everyone can become more efficient. And this is especially true at the Naval Academy where you are expected to be top notch students, athletes and officers-in-training simultaneously.

But time management is not the cure-all of academic difficulties. This manual covers all the basic study skills necessary for academic success. The chapters cover motivation, time management, note taking, reading, test taking and anxiety management as well as other resources available.

The trail of academic success passes the landmarks of motivation, selection, modification and application. Students must first be motivated to start the change process. As you cover the material in this manual, actively select that which is most relevant to your situation, then modify the material to fit your specific needs. The final step toward academic success is application. All the skills in the world will be worthless if you do not attempt to use them. You can be successful and become an "Attack Student". Begin now to take an active role in your own education.

Academic Effectiveness:

A Manual for Scholastic Success at the United States Naval Academy

Fourth Edition

C H A P T E R

O N E

GETTING STARTED

CHAPTER OUTLINE

- Academics at the Naval Academy

- Personal Goals and Motivation

- Learning Styles

- Tips to Success at the Naval Academy

Most midshipmen never experience major academic difficulties before they come to the academy. Each new class of midshipmen is composed of some of the most talented young men and women in America. For example, the Class of 1997 average SAT scores were 570 (verbal) and 667 (math) for a combined SAT score of 1237. Eighty percent of the class were in the upper fifth of their secondary school classes. There is no question that the Naval Academy selects some of the best young people that America has to offer. At first glance, one might think that midshipmen should not be having any problems with academics. But such is not the case. Each semester many midshipmen struggle with the fact that they seem to be working as hard as possible yet receive lower grades than they have ever received before. They are continuously faced with the frustration of hearing that friends at civilian schools are working less and receiving better grades.

Midshipmen soon realize that something must change. However, the heavy academic and military demands will not be reduced. It is important that students realize that the only place where change is going to occur is within themselves. But awareness is only the first step. Changing behavior that has developed over the past 12 to 15 years is not easy.

Beginning with the Class of 1994, almost all midshipman have been administered a study skills questionnaire. The questionnaires have been designed to evaluate behavior related to academic performance. During Plebe Summer, your Academic Adviser may have given you a copy of your study skills profile. If you do not have your own copy you can get your copy or arrange to take the questionnaire by calling the Academic Center located in Ward Hall (X35281). Advisers are available in the Academic Center to interpret the study skills results so that you can focus on those areas which you report to be the most difficult.

ACADEMICS AT THE NAVAL ACADEMY

As most midshipmen know, academics at the Naval Academy are not the only "master". At times it seems as though academics are not even the most important priority. The professional topics taught in Bancroft and Luce Halls are the very essence of what make the Naval Academy different from civilian colleges. To neglect this material is to ensure that there will be problems ahead. Yet, to neglect your academics is an even quicker way to ensure failure and potential separation from the Academy.

PERSONAL GOALS AND MOTIVATION

The clues to success at the Naval Academy begin with personal goals. The answers to better performance here at the Academy are rooted in some of the most basic questions related to your being a midshipman at the Naval Academy. The questions in Exercise 1-1 should be addressed regularly throughout your academic career in order to ensure that you are on track and to help you realize again why you have chosen to attend the United States Naval Academy.

Exercise 1-1: WHY ARE YOU HERE?

Why did you choose to come to a military academy instead of a civilian college? As specifically as you can, write down why *YOU* made this decision.

_____

_____

_____

_____

Why did you choose the Naval Academy over West Point, the Air Force or Coast Guard? Again, try to write down your own reasons for choosing the Naval Academy.

_____

_____

_____

_____

What are the reasons you have stayed at the Naval Academy this long? There probably have been many times since I-Day when you wondered why you were staying here. Use this part of the exercise to elaborate why you have chosen to stay when you most felt like separating.

_____

_____

_____

_____

Exercise 1-1 was designed to help you look at what motivates or drives you to stay at the Academy. Now that you have thought about why you are here, consider how being here relates to your life goals.

Exercise 1-2 LIFE VALUES

Take a few minutes to think about the meaning to you of the items listed below and then rank order the items according to which are more or less important to you. Rank the most important item as #1, the next most important item as #2, etc.

____ Self-sufficiency	____ Influence	____ Power
____ Receiving love	____ Giving Love	____ Travel
____ Spontaneity	____ Adventure	____ Health
____ A large family	____ Spiritual fulfillment	____ Approval
____ Solitude	____ Prestige	____ Wealth
____ A close and supportive family	____ Intellectual stimulation	

In the space provided below, briefly relate the top ten items to your continued attendance at the Naval Academy in order from strongest to weakest. Is there a close relationship to those items that are most important to you and your perseverance here?

_____	_____
_____	_____
_____	_____
_____	_____
_____	_____

How important are these goals in comparison to being commissioned in the Navy or Marine Corps?

_____

_____

_____

It is also important to have some idea about how you learn and what specific learning situations are best suited to you. You may not be able to change the learning environment, but with the knowledge of your own preferred learning styles, you should be better able to deal with the situations with which you are faced.

The following section on learning styles was written by CDR Maureen Sullivan and is adapted from the information she has developed for the Academic Effectiveness courses taught in the Academic Center.

LEARNING STYLES

Socrates' adage "know thyself" still rings true as we approach the 21st century. In fact, awareness of your strengths and weaknesses as a student will serve as a vital foundation to manage your academic performance. There are many approaches to studying and learning. Some students are very energetic in the morning while others prefer to study late into the evening. Some students require privacy and silence to concentrate when they read while others prefer background music or an environment with "low" noise. Just as an athlete develops his or her optimum training schedule, you can improve your study skills based on your natural learning style.

In the following space, write your full name as you normally do:

#1 _____

Now, write your full name on line #2 using your other hand:

#2 _____

What are some adjectives you would use to describe writing your name on line #1? How would you describe the experience of writing your name on line #2?

_____

_____

_____

_____

Typically, students respond with the following descriptors or their equivalent for each of the tasks:

#1	#2
Easy	Awkward
Natural	Uncomfortable
Comfortable	Difficult
Don't have to think about it	Hard
Effortless	Have to concentrate

The major difference appears to be that task #1 is the student's natural way of writing while task #2 is not. The important point to remember is that you can still write your name both ways. However, the task #2 way requires much more effort and time, and does not produce the same quality as task #1.

Sometimes, studying yields outcomes similar to those listed in task #2 when you are not attuned to your learning style.

In another example, if I am speaking Spanish to you and you only understand English, how effective will our communication be? The communication process requires a transmitter and a receiver that are synchronized so a message can be effectively transmitted and received. The process of learning involves communication. If you are not effectively receiving the message that is transmitted via your instructor or another medium, your success may depend on extra effort to understand the message through other learning strategies such as reviewing other students' notes, meeting for extra instruction with a professor and experimenting with other resources. Most study methods can eventually enhance your success as a student but some will be more compatible with your natural learning style.

Learning Modalities

As a student you are constantly exposed to a variety of information that is presented via different formats. Teachers may require you to view a movie, listen to a lecture, read a book or perform a lab to stimulate your understanding of the material that they are presenting to you. All information that you receive and process is initially perceived through your senses. One theory of learning suggests that there are three major sensory forms of learning: auditory, kinesthetic and visual.

Which modality best describes your style of acquiring information? The *auditory* learner acquires information most easily through hearing and verbalization. The *kinesthetic* learner is most successful when a physical approach, such as writing or doing, is involved. The *visual* learner processes information best through sight.

Auditory Learners Tend to Learn Best When They:

- Hear verbal instructions.
- Obtain information that is presented on an audiotape.
- Participate in a lecture or a class discussion not merely textbook reading.
- Vocalize what they have read.

Kinesthetic Learners Tend to Learn Best When They:

- Are physically involved in a learning experience such as a lab, exercise or an activity that requires hands-on involvement.
- Can take a theory and demonstrate it via an experiment or project.
- Can use several senses simultaneously to maximize their interaction to acquire new information (e.g., computer note-taking).
- Can touch objects or experience events they are learning about.

Visual Learners Tend to Learn Best When They:

- See information through reading, videotapes, movies, or overhead visuals.
- Observe photographs or other graphics that represent theoretical information.

As you may already know, teachers do not routinely teach to one modality, or at any rate, only your preferred learning style. However, by knowing your preferred learning modality, you are empowered to focus on your strengths and to develop your weaknesses. If we review the initial exercise in this section, this is where it applies. You CAN write with your other hand with practice and obtain some pretty successful results.

The following techniques are aids for strengthening each of the three learning modalities.

Auditory Learners Can:

- Use a tape recorder to record and review information.
- Select an oral assignment when options are available.
- Study in a group where there is a verbal exchange of information.
- Teach other students information through a verbal description.

Kinesthetic Learners Can:

- Use computers to record or review notes.
- Participate in laboratory exercises or volunteer to perform concrete projects that will demonstrate textbook information.
- Study facts in combination with a physical activity (e.g., reading notecards while working out on a stairclimber).
- Write information on flashcards and review the cards while walking around.

Visual Learners Can:

- Use a variety of visual aids such as different colored pens, highlighters, diagrams, drawings, graphs, etc. for effective note-taking.
- Review the textbook before class.
- Scan notes periodically since many visual learners actually remember whether information was on the left or right side of their notebook or textbook.
- Draw special symbols that will serve as memory joggers.

Experimenting with some of these techniques to filter and process new information will assist you in organizing and associating the information for easier access by you. Remember that study habits are also learned and ineffective ones can be unlearned to make way for more efficient strategies.

OK, you now have some idea of your study skills strengths and weaknesses and you have had a chance to think about your preferred learning style, and your personal goals are in order. The following section, "Tips to Success at the Naval Academy", should prove helpful as you move toward academic effectiveness.

The following comments were collected from midshipmen. They are most often verbatim, and should prove to be helpful to you as you get started on the road to academic effectiveness. They serve well as a transition to the next chapter, Time Management.

TIPS TO SUCCESS AT THE NAVAL ACADEMY

1. Sit in the front row, and pay attention in class. Make sure you grasp basic concepts as you go along—ask questions on what you don't understand.

2. Start working hard the very first day. Don't fall behind.

3. Arrange for extra instruction (EI) if you start falling behind or as you become confused—at the first sign of difficulty.

4. Do all the assignment before going to class—skim for major points then read for details.

5. Don't rely on studying old tests—they are an aid but not the answer.

6. Participate in class—don't let anything go by that you don't understand.

7. Stay awake. Stand if necessary. Act interested.

8. Study subjects you like later than the ones you don't.

9. Take good notes in class. They help you understand what the professor wants. Organize your notes as soon as possible after class. Fill in the blanks.

10. Learn from questions asked by others. Pay attention to what is going on.

11. Study and review with others. Begin your review for exams at least one week before the exam date.

12. Be sure to copy down problem types and examples given in class.

C H A P T E R

T W O

TIME MANAGEMENT

CHAPTER OUTLINE

- Semester Schedule

- Weekly Schedule

- Creating Your Own Time Management System

- Daily Schedule

C hapter One, "Getting Started," had several exercises designed to help you focus on your own personal reasons for being at the Naval Academy. Now that you have spent some time thinking about why you are here, it is time to begin to ensure that you get to stay here. The way you use your time and energy can make a big difference in your effectiveness and efficiency as a student.

Recently a group of midshipmen was asked to describe the biggest obstacle to their academic performance. The overwhelming response was *TIME*. Most midshipmen believe that if there was just more time, everything could be accomplished. There is little likelihood that you will ever get more time, and little likelihood that the statement is true. The truth is, there probably is not enough time to do everything you want. However, there is usually enough time to do those things which midshipmen are required to do, and most of what you are allowed to do. There are 168 hours in a week. That does not change. You cannot find more hours in the week to do all you want or need to do. But you can learn to use your time more effectively. You can learn to work more efficiently.

The purpose of this chapter is to offer some suggestions for more effective use of time. These techniques have been shown to be helpful to many people here at the Naval Academy as well as in military, educational and business settings throughout the world.

There are three levels of time management upon which this chapter will focus: semester, weekly and daily. In order to be most effective in your use of time, it is important that you learn to take control of each level. The first focus will be on the semester schedule.

SEMESTER SCHEDULE

In order to get the most out of the short amount of time that there is in a semester, it is important to be able to have a "big picture" of your semester requirements. Use the calendar provided at the end of this chapter to map out your semester. It might help to use color coding to mark off academic reserve periods, holidays and any leave time. Use your course syllabuses to help you fill in all your major assignments. Be sure to use pencil so that you can change the schedule if the assignment dates change. This should give an overall view of what you can expect for the semester. It is important to note that all schedules must allow for flexibility. Many assignments change as the semester evolves. You may find that a particular assignment takes less time than you had predicted or that you may change the topic for a term paper and need to spend more time than you had originally thought.

Whatever the situation, be ready to make adjustments in your schedules. Make copies of your semester schedule to keep with all your class notebooks. This will enable you to keep on top of your assignments and chart your progress throughout the semester.

WEEKLY SCHEDULE

The next level of time management is the weekly schedule. An important move toward more effective use of your time is to see that there really is time available to you. Begin to get control of your time by filling in one of the blank weekly schedules provided at the end of this chapter. Several steps are listed below which should be helpful in this process. A filled-out schedule is provided at the end of this chapter as an example.

Creating Your Own Time Management System

1. Fill in all your classes and labs. This is *inflexible* time that is already dedicated to your academics.

2. Block off the 0630–0755 time Monday–Friday. This is time spent getting ready for the day. For plebes, the time is usually devoted to studying rates.

3. Block off the time usually devoted to varsity or brigade athletics or drill practice. This is usually 1530–1830, Monday–Friday.

4. Count up the time unaccounted for. Include the open hours during the day, as well as on weekends. The total time should amount to about 35 or 40 hours or more, depending on the number of courses you are taking.

5. Decide how many hours you need to study per week for each course. If you don't think you can estimate the necessary study time, a common "rule of thumb" is to plan for two hours of study for each credit hour. For example, if you are taking SC104 for four hours credit, you can expect to have to study about eight hours per week for that course. At the Naval Academy, semester credit hours usually range between 17 and 20. That means that the ideal number of study hours per week will be somewhere between 34 and 40. Remember, this is just an estimate. You will need to make changes as the course demands change. Of course, each person will have to determine how many hours of study are necessary for his or her own requirements. Use the table below to tabulate your weekly study hours.

COURSE	TITLE	HOURS	STUDY HOURS
_____	_____	_____	_____
_____	_____	_____	_____
_____	_____	_____	_____
_____	_____	_____	_____
_____	_____	_____	_____
_____	_____	_____	_____
_____	_____	_____	_____

Total Study Hours per week: _____

6. Read the following scheduling suggestions and then decide when you are going to study what.

(a) Don't allow yourself 10–15 minutes to "warm up" before studying. Get right down to business and stay at it for at least 30 minutes and for not more than one and one half hours at a time. Research has shown that alertness is likely to decline dramatically after 30 minutes or so of hard mental work.

(b) Take breaks of 5–10 minutes after every one hour study session. Reward yourself for doing a good job with a stretch, a bite to eat, some pleasure reading, etc., during these breaks. Make sure to keep the breaks short and sweet. Make the breaks at meaningful places (such as at the end of a chapter) rather than at an arbitrary time period.

(c) Some of the best times to study are immediately after a lecture class and immediately before a discussion class. Use the time between classes to study as much as you can.

(d) If possible, try to arrange your schedule so that you study the same subject at the same time each day. It is much better to study a subject every day at the same time than to have occasional long sessions. This daily routine develops habits that facilitate getting down to work and concentrating.

Now it is time to fill in the blanks. Go ahead and fill in your weekly study hours.

DAILY SCHEDULE

The next level of time management to be covered pertains to your daily schedule. Most successful business executives and military leaders spend a few minutes at the end of each day getting organized for the next day. You should find that the few minutes spent in this manner is a very small investment with a high return. The investment of five to ten minutes at the end of each day can save you hours and even days of wasted time trying to figure out what you should be doing.

First use your weekly schedule to find out what you had originally planned for the day. Then review the semester schedule to see if you need to work on any long term assignments or study for any tests. You can now prepare a to-do list for the following day. Use a 3 X 5 note card to list your classes on one side and your to-do list on the other. This daily schedule is something you can carry with you throughout the day as a reminder of what you have planned to do. It can also help you be more aware of things that you are not doing or of study time that is being disrupted. This information is critical for self diagnosis. You should be able to pinpoint your own study problems as they arise.

This chapter has covered three levels of time management: semester schedules, weekly schedules and daily schedules. Now the hard part begins. In order for the schedules to be helpful, they must be used. You will find that if you follow a realistic, flexible schedule you will be able to do all of what you are required to do and most of what you are allowed to do.

The next chapter, "Classroom Note-Taking," will teach you several techniques for improving your effectiveness in classroom situations.

1998 Sunday	Monday	Tuesday	AUGUST Wednesday	Thursday	Friday	1998 Saturday
						1
2	3	4	5	6	7	8
9	10	11	12	13	14	15
16	17	18	19	20	21	22
23 / 30	24 / 31	25	26	27	28	29

SEPTEMBER

Sunday	Monday	Tuesday	Wednesday	Thursday	Friday	Saturday
		1	2	3	4	5
6	7	8	9	10	11	12
13	14	15	16	17	18	19
20	21	22	23	24	25	26
27	28	29	30			

OCTOBER

Sunday	Monday	Tuesday	Wednesday	Thursday	Friday	Saturday
				1	2	3
4	5	6	7	8	9	10
11	12	13	14	15	16	17
18	19	20	21	22	23	24
25	26	27	28	29	30	31

NOVEMBER

Sunday	Monday	Tuesday	Wednesday	Thursday	Friday	Saturday
1	2	3	4	5	6	7
8	9	10	11	12	13	14
15	16	17	18	19	20	21
22	23	24	25	26	27	28
29	30					

DECEMBER

Sunday	Monday	Tuesday	Wednesday	Thursday	Friday	Saturday
		1	2	3	4	5
6	7	8	9	10	11	12
13	14	15	16	17	18	19
20	21	22	23	24	25	26
27	28	29	30	31		

1999 Sunday	Monday	Tuesday	JANUARY Wednesday	Thursday	Friday	1999 Saturday
					1	2
3	4	5	6	7	8	9
10	11	12	13	14	15	16
17	18	19	20	21	22	23
24 31	25	26	27	28	29	30

FEBRUARY

	1	2	3	4	5	6
7	8	9	10	11	12	13
14	15	16	17	18	19	20
21	22	23	24	25	26	27
28						

MARCH

	1	2	3	4	5	6
7	8	9	10	11	12	13
14	15	16	17	18	19	20
21	22	23	24	25	26	27
28	29	30	31			

APRIL

				1	2	3
4	5	6	7	8	9	10
11	12	13	14	15	16	17
18	19	20	21	22	23	24
25	26	27	28	29	30	

MAY

						1
2	3	4	5	6	7	8
9	10	11	12	13	14	15
16	17	18	19	20	21	22
23 30	24 31	25	26	27	28	29

WEEKLY SCHEDULE

	Sunday	Monday	Tuesday	Wednesday	Thursday	Friday	Saturday
0630							
0755							
0855				BREAKFAST			
0955							1015
1055							
1330				LUNCH			
1430							
1530							
1630							
1700				DINNER			
1800							
1930							
2000							
2100							
2200							
2300							0100

Schedules designed by Mr. Thomas Schulze at the USNA Academic Center.

WEEKLY SCHEDULE

	Sunday	Monday	Tuesday	Wednesday	Thursday	Friday	Saturday
0630							
0755				BREAKFAST			
0855							
0955							1015
1055							
1330				LUNCH			
1430							
1530							
1630							
1700							
1930	1800			DINNER			
2000							
2100							
2200							
2300							0100

WEEKLY SCHEDULE

	Sunday	Monday	Tuesday	Wednesday	Thursday	Friday	Saturday
0630							
0755			*BREAKFAST*				
0855							
0955							1015
1055							
1330				*LUNCH*			
1430							
1530							
1630							
1700							
1800	1800			*DINNER*			
1930							
2000							
2100							
2200							
2300							0100

WEEKLY SCHEDULE

Sunday Monday Tuesday Wednesday Thursday Friday Saturday

BREAKFAST

LUNCH

DINNER

1015

1800

0100

0630
0755
0855
0955
1055
1330
1430
1530
1630
1700
1930
2000
2100
2200
2300

WEEKLY SCHEDULE

Time	Sunday	Monday	Tuesday	Wednesday	Thursday	Friday	Saturday
0630		Come Arounds and Daily Prep →				→	
0755		Prep for FP	NL	BREAKFAST	NL	Prep for FP	
0855		FP	Study NL	FP	Prep for GM	FP	
0955		GM	Errands	GM	GM	GM	1015
1055		Pro Topics	PE	Pro Topics			
				LUNCH			
1330	Study Calc.	HE	Chem Lab	HE	EI	HE	
1430	Study Calc.	GC	Chem Lab	GC	EI	GC	
1530	Study Chem.	Sports & Drill				↑	
1630	Study Chem.	↓				↑	
1700				DINNER			
1800	1800						
1930	Study NL	Study Chem	Study Calc	Study HE	Study FP	Study HE	
2000	Study Chem	(Chem Lab?)	Study Calc	Study Chem	Study Calc	Study FP	
2100	Study Chem	Study HE	Study FP	Study Chem	Study HE		
2200	Study Calc	Study HE	Study FP	Study NL	Study HE		
2300							0100

C H A P T E R

THREE

CLASSROOM NOTE-TAKING

CHAPTER OUTLINE

➡ Before the Lecture

➡ During the Lecture

➡ After the Lecture

➡ The Cornell Note-Taking System

➡ Listening and Note-Taking Skills

➡ How to Study Mathematics

A major portion of each midshipman's weekday is spent in the classroom. It seems logical that most students would know how to use classroom time effectively. Unfortunately, such is not the case. Many students at the Naval Academy spend much of their classroom time either drifting off or attempting to take verbatim notes. Neither behavior shows the most effective use of class time. This chapter will provide you with several techniques proven to be valuable for recording and retaining lecture material. This is a critical step toward becoming a more successful student.

Lecture note-taking can be divided into three main time units; the time before class, during class and after class. What you do in each of these time units can make a critical difference in how well you retain and recall important material from the lecture. The ability to retain and recall is directly related to your academic performance.

BEFORE THE LECTURE

Your mental state or mind set before you enter the classroom can make the difference between really understanding the material presented in class and leaving the classroom at the end of the period feeling as though you were in the wrong class. Knowing in advance what the professor is going to talk about, or at least what you think is going to be covered, will help you to understand the material better. If you have been able to find the thread of information that usually connects most lectures, the material will make more sense to you. When the material makes sense to you, it is often easier to be retained and recalled at a later date.

The best way to try to be prepared for the present is to *review the past*. What was the professor talking about at the last lecture? What were the unanswered questions that need to be clarified in the present lecture? It only takes a few minutes to skim the previous class notes in an attempt to predict what is going to be covered in the present lecture. Spend the few minutes before each class going over the notes from the last lecture. Note any unfinished explanations. Be able to respond accurately when the professor says "Let's see, where did we end last time?"

Skimming your notes before class is valuable for several reasons. First, it refreshes your memory. It is one more time of going over the material. For most people, learning takes place primarily through repetition. Skimming lecture notes before class also allows you to respond in class with understanding. Equally important, quickly reviewing your notes can get your mind ready for what is coming next. By going over previous lecture notes just before class, you are establishing anchor points for new information. Each lecture is then linked to the preceding lecture and it becomes easier for you to discern the threads that tie the class together. Once you have your "mind set" right, you are ready for the period during the lecture.

DURING THE LECTURE

In high school, most students take minimal class notes. Most of the time listening in class is enough to do well. However, the Naval Academy is not high school. You need to do more than just show up for class. You need to take notes in order to perform as well as possible.

Research has shown that adults will routinely forget approximately 50% of the material presented in a lecture when they are tested immediately after the lecture (Pauk, 1989). The rate of forgetting continues to increase as time goes on. It is interesting to note that there is evidence to suggest that students who take notes in class tend to do worse when tested immediately after class than students who actively listened. That may be why many students decide not to take class notes. They often claim that taking notes interferes with their ability to understand what the lecture is about. Depending on the type of note taking and the type of material being covered, taking notes can interfere with understanding the material. Attempting to take verbatim notes often does interfere with understanding. In some courses it is more important to *ACTIVELY* listen instead of attempting to take everything down.

However, in most college level courses, it would be highly unusual for a professor to test students immediately after the lecture. It is more likely that testing will occur days, weeks and even months after the material has been presented. It then becomes very important that students have some form of notes for study. Deep learning takes place after the lecture.

AFTER THE LECTURE

> *Referring to notes after the material has been presented is the most important of the three time segments being covered.*

As soon as possible after the lecture is over, spend a few minutes going over the new material. Not only is this another opportunity to cover the material, it is also a way to check the legibility of your notes and mark any point that needs to be clarified at the next lecture. You can additionally use the time to straighten up your notes if they are a little disorganized and correct any errors that you notice.

Now that we have discussed the time before, during and after the lecture, it is important to have an organized system of note-taking which will enable you to perform most effectively in these three units of time. It is fortunate that there is already an established system available for you. One of the most used note taking techniques was developed by Professor William Pauk, the Director of the Reading Research Center at Cornell University. The technique, known as the "Cornell Note-Taking System" is described below.

This note-taking system consists of a specific format and five steps. The format consists of 8½ x 11 loose leaf notebook paper with a vertical line drawn 2½ inches from the left. Classroom notes are taken in the right hand column and the 2½ inch column on the left is for recall. Once the note sheet is partitioned, you are ready to start taking notes. Use the five steps listed on the following page to take more accurate lecture notes.

THE CORNELL NOTE-TAKING SYSTEM

1. **RECORD**

   During the lecture, record in the main column as many meaningful facts and ideas as you can. Write legibly. Use a simple form and your own words. A modified outline is often helpful here. Try to use the instructor's exact words only for definitions and technical terms. Use abbreviations whenever possible, but be sure to include a key to your abbreviations to help you translate later.

2. **REDUCE**

   As soon after the lecture as possible, reduce or summarize the main ideas and facts concisely in the recall column. Summarizing clarifies meanings and relationships, reinforces continuity and strengthens memory. It is also a way of preparing for examinations gradually and well ahead of time.

3. **RECITE**

   Now cover the main column. Using only your notes in the recall column as cues. State the facts and ideas of the lecture as fully as you can. Do this in your own words. Then uncover the notes to verify what you have said. This helps transfer the facts and ideas into your long term memory.

4. **REFLECT**

   Reflection is thinking. Merely learning the facts is not enough to do well at the Naval Academy. Midshipmen must take a deeper step into learning by thinking about and trying to apply course material. Reflective students ask questions about the material in an attempt to acquire a deeper understanding. Keeping and reviewing notes about your own thoughts and opinions about the material will help you think critically about the information you have received in class. Consider keeping a journal of your reflections about the material in your courses.

5. **REVIEW**

   Every day provides new information. Each new bit of information can interfere with previously learned material. The best way to ensure that you do not forget is to review on a regular basis. If you spend 10 minutes every week in a quick review of your notes, you will retain most of what you have learned, and you will be able to use your knowledge more effectively.

(adapted from material presented in *How to Study in College* by Walter Pauk)

An essential element of any effective note-taking system is listening. The Air Force Academy has developed a list of important listening skills that apply equally well at the Naval Academy. A sincere thanks to our colleagues at the Air Force Academy for sharing the information on the next page.

Many students are under the false impression that the closer their notes are to the actual words used by the lecturer, the better they are. To them, quantity of notes and exact wording are all important. Actually, good notes depend on two entirely different factors: (1) selection, and (2) organization.

LISTENING AND NOTE-TAKING SKILLS

Good listening is an *active* process. Listening, like reading, involves active concentration and continuous evaluation. Listening is an active continuous connecting of what is said, with what you have heard and believed. Listening requires organization for future use. To improve your listening skills and note taking ability, try the following suggestions.

1. Prepare for Listening

- Read your notes from previous lectures.
- Read the assignment on which the lecture will be given.
- Arrive early, sit where you can see and hear, and be seen and be heard.
- Have your notebook, pencils, and other materials at hand.
- Formulate questions you want answered.
- Write the questions down!

2. Listen and Write

- Attend critically to all that is said. Sort out the main ideas.
- Know your professors, their values and their thought processes.
- Write neatly, abbreviate freely, symbolize quickly. Create your own list or key to abbreviations and symbols.
- Outline, indent, leave space.
- Relate in writing and in thoughts.
- Question continuously.

3. Review

- Immediately after class, review your notes and fill in what you missed during the lecture.
- If necessary, reorganize your notes.
- Try to predict from the lecture what questions will be on the test, on what you need to concentrate.

4. Use Notes Effectively

- Review before lecture, before reading assignment, before tests.
- Let your mind be free to visualize concepts and relationships.

(adapted with permission from the United States Air Force Academy How To Study Program)

Your first task is to select critically from the statements made by the lecturer those which are most essential to your understanding of the topic being discussed. Your second task is to organize these facts or statements in some meaningful fashion which you will be able to use at a later date. Both of these tasks require understanding and reasoning that cannot be attained mechanically.

In brief, learning requires action—active listening and thinking.

This chapter has focused on the time before, during, and after class. What is most important to remember from this chapter is that it is critical that you take notes in class. The notes need to be thorough as well as legible. Any note taking system is worthless if it cannot be used for later review. As with all the study skills discussed in this book, the Cornell System works, but only if it is used.

Throughout the last few years, several students have asked if there are study techniques that are specifically valuable in mathematics or technical courses. The following information was provided by Associate Professor Richard Maruszewski, a Mathematics professor at the Naval Academy.

How to Study Mathematics

The principles given elsewhere in this manual are pertinent to math courses as well, but there are several study techniques that are especially important for ideas more specific to your math courses. Let's begin by giving some general rules for success.

> RULE 1: Always do your class assignments.
> RULE 2: Be an active participant during class.
>
> WHEN ALL ELSE FAILS: See RULE 1.

Math teachers often wear a pin that states, "Math is not a spectator sport." This pin and the rules above accentuate the same idea. The best way to learn mathematics is to do it yourself. You can not expect to learn to play the piano or learn to play basketball by only watching concerts or basketball games. Likewise, you can not expect to learn mathematics by going to class but never actually working the problems. You must become an active participant in order to succeed in your math courses.

Math Classes

Learning how to do math begins with the class itself. Always come to class prepared to take notes. Although the level of detail and the quantity of the notes will differ from student to student, it is always a good practice to begin by taking extensive, detailed notes and reduce the amount as needed. Most instructors will present material differently than the book does. Record at least the main ideas for future reference. Always take notes about problems the instructor works out. There is a good chance that you will see that problem type again. An additional side benefit to taking good class notes is that it automatically makes you more active. The more active you are the more alert you will be.

Ask questions when you are confused. If you have a question, many of your fellow students will probably have the same question. You will be helping them as well as yourself. Asking questions will also help you to be more alert and more active. In a similar vein, do not get too comfortable. If you are getting drowsy, stand up and go to the back of the room. But remember, take your notes with you. You can take notes and ask questions from the back of the room as well. Finally, make sure that you can see the board clearly from your seat. If you can't see clearly, change seats.

Most instructors understand that you won't completely finish every assignment every night. Instructors know that you are taking other courses which also put demands on your time. However, never skip an assignment completely. Give math at least some time each night. It will be much harder to fill in the gaps later when you do not remember the class as well. Begin your assignment by reviewing your notes. Fill in whatever you did not completely finish in class. If necessary, rewrite them. Your notes will make much more sense to you later in the day that you took them than they will a month later, on the night before the test. Pay special attention to the examples the instructor worked in class. These examples were chosen because they illustrate important concepts. Now work as much of the assignment as time allows. If you cannot finish the assignment, don't just work the first group of problems. The assignment covers more than one type of problem, so working only the first few might result in serious gaps in your learning. Work every second problem or every third problem or whatever, but remember, your goal is to complete the assignment. If you do better by participating in a study group, try to find one that suits you. Some teachers will collect and correct homework. Some will never look at the assignments. Don't let grading policies deter you. Prepare each night with the assumption that the next class will start with a quiz.

When in doubt, consult RULE 1.

Finally, if you identify weak points as you work on your assignment, try to clear them up with questions in the next class or go to your instructor as soon as possible for help outside of class.

Absences From Class

If for some reason you miss a class, remember that it is your responsibility to recover the lost material. You cannot expect your instructor to re-teach a class to you. Find a classmate who takes good notes. (Your instructor may be able to recommend one.) Rewrite these notes in your own style so that they will blend well with the ones that you took in other classes. Read the section covered in this book. Do the homework as previously suggested. If problems arise, go to see your instructor and ask precise, well thought out questions. Don't be surprised to find out that it takes much more time to make up a class than it does to go to one.

Preparing for Tests

When it comes time for the test, your daily work will pay off. You will have a good set of notes which include examples. You will also have plenty of example problems that you have worked yourself. You will not have to do an all nighter, and you will have more time to see the bigger picture. When you do review problems for the test, mix them up rather than doing one section at a time. Some students do very well working problems in a single section because they know what approach that section calls for, but when problems are mixed as on a test, they have difficulty selecting the correct approach.

Math tests are usually a cross between objective and essay tests. You will seldom be given a true/false or multiple choice question, and essay questions are also rather rare. You will be asked to come up with "the one correct solution along with your supporting work. Also be ready to explain and answer questions about your solution in good English. Write all of your work, as legibly as possible. Do not try to conserve paper. The easier it is for your instructor to read your work, the more likely it is that you will receive fullest possible credit.

When you review for the final exam, again use your notes and assignments and now also your hourly tests as your base. Try to see major areas covered by the course. There will be lots of trees. Look for the forest. The main ideas are what you will take with you to your future work. The details can be relearned later as appropriate. Again in practice sessions, mix problems. There will be a lot of different concepts to mix. The author of the final may be someone other than your instructor, so be ready to see a slightly different form of test. Otherwise, prepare as for an hourly test.

CHAPTER FOUR

READING EFFECTIVENESS

CHAPTER OUTLINE

➥ Increasing Reading Speed

➥ SQ3R Reading Method

➥ Timed Reading Sample

Chapter Three focused on the time students spend in class. A great deal of learning takes place in class. Training yourself to be more efficient in the classroom is very important. However, even more time is spent out of class. A large part of all students' time is taken up by reading. This chapter focuses on this most critical aspect of the learning process.

Because of the extensive screening that takes place before an individual is admitted to the Naval Academy, all midshipmen have acquired at least a basic reading competency. However, one of the most common complaints from midshipmen is that they are not able to keep up with all the reading assignments. They often report difficulty with *reading speed, concentration, comprehension,* or *retention.* What appears to be a contradiction is explained by the fact that although all midshipmen have learned to read, few have learned to read effectively.

When midshipmen come to the Academic Center asking for help because of reading problems, they usually begin by stating that they cannot complete all their reading assignments. They complain that they read too slowly. With questioning, they often describe situations where they have read several pages of an assignment before realizing that their thoughts were on something other than the assignment at hand. Their eyes have covered the words but very little remains in their memory. Not only do they read slowly, they also have problems with concentration. They report that they do not understand the material and they have difficulty remembering what they cannot understand.

It usually turns out that the problem is related to passive versus active reading. If students can learn to read more actively, if they learn to push themselves more, they will find that concentration increases. They begin to pay more attention to what they are reading. As they pay more attention they understand more and consequently retain more. In learning, everything is connected.

This chapter discusses all four problem areas that many midshipmen report. The chapter starts with a section on increasing reading speed, one of the main causes of concentration problems.

The section on reading speed is followed by a discussion of a reading technique that has been thoroughly researched. The technique, called the *SQ3R Method,* has been shown to increase comprehension and retention. With practice the SQ3R Method will also help increase reading speed.

> **Increased comprehension plus increased retention plus increased speed equals increased reading effectiveness**

INCREASING READING SPEED

An important first question to ask is, "Should I try to increase my reading speed?" The answer is, "It depends." It depends on how fast you are presently reading, how fast you want to read, and what material you are reading for what purpose.

The average high school graduate reads about 225 words per minute (wpm) while the average college graduate reads about 300 wpm. You can test your own reading speed by setting a timer for one minute and start reading at your natural speed. Count the number of words you have covered at the end of one minute. If you wish to test yourself, a reading passage from **Fundamentals of Naval Leadership** is provided for you at the end of this chapter. If you are reading considerably below 300 wpm, you may want to begin to push yourself while you read so that you begin to read phrases instead of individual words.

The following suggestions were provided by Mr. Lewis Fleischner of Learning Skills, Inc.

There is evidence that concentration and comprehension increase as reading rate goes up, provided that the rate technique is methodologically sound.

To read faster you need to realize that rate is not dependent on the speed of eye motion, but is controlled by the number of focal *stops* you make. If there are 12 words on a line, and you need to focus on each word, you will necessarily be reading more slowly than someone who can absorb two, three, or four words per focal stop.

Word-by-word readers need to train themselves to move from focal vision reading to peripheral vision reading. Since the eye's focal field has dominance over its peripheral field, this requires that you empty your focal field. Literally, you must train yourself to "read between the lines", focusing your eyes *above* the words rather than on the words. By looking at the blank space between the lines of print, you are effectively emptying your focal field, thereby allowing your peripheral field to become active over a group of words.

To insure good comprehension at these higher rates it is necessary that the number of words you absorb with one focal stop is a coherent group, i.e. a grammatical unit, a phrase. To train yourself to read by phrases, take a 10 line passage and divide it into its phrase structure as illustrated:

STEP I:

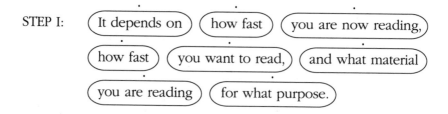

Each phrase should be encircled and a focal dot placed centrally above it. After parsing 10 lines in this manner, return to the start of the passage and move your eyes from focal dot to focal dot above each prepared phrase group, letting your peripheral field work to absorb the number of words in the enclosing circles. At first, you may find this somewhat "choppy", but with exercise you will see the material smooth out and become continuous.

Once you feel you can see and understand the content of each phrase, reduce the exercise format in stages:

STEP II: /=˙==/ =˙=/ =˙=/==˙==/ (dot & divider)

STEP III: == =˙= == =˙ ==˙= == (only central dot)

As you progress from exercise level to exercise level, you are approaching phrase reading as a method. Once your eye and brain are coordinated in this manner (eye: peripheral field; brain: phrase recognition) the technique takes over and you will find that you can read through pages much more rapidly than before (though it doesn't *feel* rapid) with much better comprehension.

Warning: never try to read an assignment and, at the same time, try to practice phrase reading. This will only divide your attention between content and method, to the detriment of both. Practice for 10 or so lines at a time (perhaps twice a day) and then do not worry about your rate method while doing your assignments. When you have developed your phrase reading skill sufficiently, it will take effect without your having to direct yourself consciously in this manner.

With practice you can learn to read faster and improve your concentration. But do not expect miraculous changes. Although there have been reports of people being taught to read thousands of words per minute, there is no scientific evidence that people can actually read that much material and retain the information.

However there is a lot of research behind the reading method described in the following section. The SQ3R Method is one of the most effective reading systems developed.

SQ3R Reading Method

SQ3R stands for *Survey—Question—Read—Recite—Review*. These steps promote an active attitude toward learning. When you clear your mind for the task of studying, you need to be alert and centered. You should be ready to learn and remember what you have covered. With practice, the following five steps will do much to improve concentration, comprehension, retention and speed.

I. SURVEY

As you begin to read a new textbook, state your purpose for reading the material. Try to come up with an answer better than "Because it is required." As you glance over the title and table of contents, look for inter-relationships. Read the forward to discover the author's point of view, and the conclusion/summary to see where the book leads. Pause and ask yourself, "What do I already know about this topic?" Skim through the Index for the largest entries (major indentations of page references). These are the main topics and people to be aware of, to take notes on, and to relate to each other when you read.

As you begin each chapter, look for a summary—usually at the beginning or end—and pick out the main points. Move on to read the section headings and if necessary, the topic sentences in the main paragraphs. Look over the Questions, Problems, Exercises at the end of the chapter to see what you should be able to do when you have finished studying. Skim over graphs, tables and illustrations to see how they support and explain the text. Check over the central ideas and relate them to your purpose for studying the material. The entire Survey of a chapter should only take a few minutes and will give you an overall framework within which to study.

II. QUESTION

Create a Question—perhaps a variation of the sub-heading—for each reading segment. This will be what guides and motivates your reading in the next step. For example, a section heading such as "Appointive Naval Leadership" can be turned into the question "What is Appointive Leadership?" This can then guide your reading in the next step.

III. READ

Read actively to answer the question you have created. Remember your original purpose for reading the material. Try using your hand or a pen to pull your eyes down the page as rapidly as you can and still understand what is being presented.

IV. RECITE

Look away from the book and attempt to answer the question from step two. What else do you remember about what you have read? If you cannot answer the question, read the section again.

> *If you can't remember what you read immediately after you have read it, you won't remember it at some future date.*

You may find it adds to your learning process to write brief phrases in outline form during the recite step. These can be used for later review. Repeat the cycle of survey, question, read, recite for each section of the assignment.

V. REVIEW

When you have completed the chapter, review any notes you have taken, look away and attempt to recite the important points of the chapter. Continue this process until you understand and know the material.

As is the case with all of the skills that are discussed in this workbook, the SQ3R Method must be used in order to be valuable to you. You will find that the it can be applied more easily to some textbooks than others. It is your task to discover what adaptations must be made for your particular situation. However, do try it out for several weeks before you attempt to evaluate its effectiveness.

The topic of this chapter has been reading. With practice, the techniques covered will help you read faster, understand better and retain more. But like all behavior, active reading must be practiced. You must actively work toward improvement in your reading. Test yourself frequently.

The next chapter will discuss what many students fear most, test taking. Test taking is often seen as the last step in the learning process, and consequently must be linked to preparation throughout the semester. However, there are also specific techniques that can improve your ability to perform at your highest level.

There are many individual differences among members of the human race. These differences make it very difficult to define what is meant by a "proper" or "normal" adjustment for an individual. A person's mental health or adjustment should be seen in terms of physical, psychological, social, moral and religious needs. All of these factors should be considered in terms of the individual's daily environment.

Any attempt to define "normal" behavior makes it apparent that the task is not an easy one. Adjustment can be thought of as the satisfaction of needs. But an individual's needs are never completely satisfied. Needs vary from person to person, and even within the same person at different times. Behavior that is quite acceptable under one set of circumstances can be completely out of order under different circumstances. For example, a person's behavior during routine training operations might not be acceptable in combat. "Normal" behavior or adjustment, then, is a matter of degree. The physician is not taken to task because he or she holds to a rather high definition of health despite the fact that the majority of people suffer from some sort of ill health. The concept of normal personality or psychological adjustment requires similar treatment.

In routine living, a people encounter many things which tend to upset their normal adjustment. They then take steps to maintain emotional equilibrium.

The human being is a needy organism born with a few primary needs. Many more needs are developed through maturity. In fact, a person's life is spent in seeking to satisfy needs.

In some situations satisfying a need is a simple process. A person with a strong need for food or rest may perform those acts found in the past to be useful in satisfying those needs. In a very simple way the need leads to familiar patterns of behavior that in turn lead to satisfaction. Everything is fine until the need returns. Then the sequence repeats itself.

When the individual can give adequate, need satisfying, responses to stimuli, life is quite simple. However, very rarely is human behavior this simple. At any one time the individual is moved not by a single need, but by multiple needs. Thus the behavior that grows out of an interacting pattern of needs is always a compromise. No single need can be fully satisfied.

(adapted from *Fundamentals of Naval Leadership*)

C
H
A
P
T
E
R

FIVE

TEST TAKING

CHAPTER OUTLINE

➡ Preparing for Exams

➡ Objective Exams

➡ Essay Exams

T hus far, this manual has covered goal setting, time management, note taking and reading. For many students, all that is left is rote repetition of the material. However, for effective students, testing is more than dumping material. It is more than the end point of a grading period. The actual act of taking an exam is only one step in the learning process. Advance preparation for exams is critical. Likewise, intelligent performance during an exam will often make the difference between success and failure.

This chapter begins with a general discussion of exam preparation. Two separate sections follow that focus on taking objective exams and essay exams.

PREPARING FOR EXAMS

There are many types and purposes of college examinations. They range from the frequent short quiz through the hour exam, mid-term and final exam. The method of preparation for each exam must be adapted to the type and purpose of the exam. A wise student starts preparing for finals the first day of classes. No amount of cramming during the final week will make up for lack of study during the semester. Careful preparation of assignments removes the necessity for the frenzied type of last minute work in which many students indulge, but does not remove the necessity for intensive review before an exam.

Systematic review is effective review.

During the week or 10 days preceding final exams, a definite schedule should be set up so that all material will be covered in several sessions rather than in one long session. In reviews just as in other types of study, short sessions are much more profitable than long drawn out cramming sessions. Reviews should be directed at integrating knowledge, since isolated facts are difficult to remember, and often meaningless. Relating your collection of facts to the major points in the course will make it much easier to remember them and make them more useful. The following is a suggested procedure for test review.

1. MAJOR TOPICS
Make a list of the major topics in the course. Skim assignment sheets, lecture notes, outlines of outside reading and quiz papers so you are sure that the list is complete.

2. SUMMARY
Write a summary or outline of related material for each of the major topics. Place particular emphasis on relationships among the topics.

3. SYSTEMATIC REVIEW
Go over the materials systematically. Apply more of your time to the subject in most need of work.

4. MOCK EXAM
Make out a set of probable questions. Keep in mind what you know about your professor's interests and points of importance. Using this mock exam is an excellent way to review after all the material has been covered.

5. REST

Adequate rest is essential. It is impossible to think clearly after an all night session of cramming. Many students find themselves unable to recall information which they had previously mastered. If at all possible, an early bedtime (before midnight) is critical for effective test performance.

6. RELAX!

Many students face every exam with such an emotional reaction that they find it impossible to demonstrate their knowledge. Avoiding last minute discussions is extremely important if you feel that excess anxiety interferes with your ability to perform. During exam week it is also wise to avoid post-exam discussions which may only give you a feeling of failure to take to the next exam.

OBJECTIVE EXAMS

Multiple choice, matching, true-false and completion exams are considered to be objective exams. They usually have one specific answer and little variation in the answer is accepted. Some specific tips to taking objective exams are listed below. Of course none of these suggestions are more important than solid advance preparation. However, once you feel you have done all you can to prepare for an exam, a certain degree of "test-wiseness" is valuable.

Taking Objective Exams

1. When reporting for an examination pay very close attention the whole time you are there. Listen very closely to all directions. Ask questions if you are in doubt. Be absolutely certain of what is expected of you. Find out if there is a penalty for guessing. Are incorrect answers weighted more than correct ones?

2. Find out exactly how much time you have and try to estimate the amount of time per question or per five questions.

3. *Read closely* and pay attention. Reading directions and listening to verbal comments about the directions are vital to answering correctly.

4. While objective exams often do not allow enough time for you to read through the whole exam twice, at least glance through it to find any sections that might be more time consuming. *Plan your time accordingly.*

5. Put off answering the more difficult or questionable items. Mark the ones you skip in the margin. Be sure and remember to return to these items before you turn in your exam.

6. Read all five choices, even when an early one seems to be the logical answer. Sometimes the fifth choice says: "All of the above", or "Two of the above", and you may only be partially correct by taking the first choice.

7. If there are five choices, read each one and cross out the choices you know to be definitely wrong. If in doubt, this narrows down the field and you stand a better chance of guessing right among two or three answers than among five.

8. Remember—almost everyone is going to miss questions. If you can avoid getting jittery over a number of missed answers and go on with a confident attitude, you will come out on top. Do not blow the exam by imagining that all is lost just because you missed what seems like a large number.

9. *Do not panic* if you see someone moving along faster than you do. If someone leaves early, he or she may have given up. Often the exams are constructed to last longer than the time given.

10. After you have left the exam room, have a debriefing with yourself. Jot down the topics covered in the exam, noting the sections of your textbooks that were covered. Note the strengths and weaknesses of your exam preparation.

11. Plan ahead to do better next time, especially in eliminating the kinds of mistakes that seem to have caused you some loss.

There are also ways to improve your performance on multiple-choice exams when your only alternative is guessing. The following suggestions are useful when all else fails.

When Studying Isn't Enough

1. You must select not only a technically correct answer, but the most *completely correct answer*. Since "all of the above" and "none of the above" are very inclusive statements, these options tend to be correct more often than would be predicted by chance alone.

2. *Be wary of options which include unqualified absolutes* such as "never," "always," "are," "guarantees," "insures." Such statements are highly restrictive and very difficult to defend. They are rarely (though they may sometimes be) correct options.

3. The less frequently stated converse of the above is that carefully qualified, conservative, or *"guarded" statements tend to be correct* more often than would be predicted by chance alone. Other things being equal, choose options containing such qualifying phrases as "may sometimes be," or "can occasionally result in."

4. Watch out for extra-long options or those with a lot of jargon. These are frequently used as decoys.

5. Use your knowledge of common prefixes, suffixes and root words to make intelligent guesses about terminology that you don't know. A knowledge of the prefix "hyper," for instance, would clue you that hypertension refers to high, not low blood pressure.

6. *Be alert to grammatical construction.* The correct answer to an item stem which ends in "an" would obviously be an option starting with a vowel. Watch also for agreement of subjects and verbs.

7. Utilize information and insights that you've acquired in working through the entire test to go back and answer earlier items of which you weren't sure.

8. If you have absolutely *NO* idea what the answer is, can't use any of the above techniques and there is no scoring penalty for guessing, choose option B or C. Studies indicate that these are correct slightly more often than would be predicted by chance alone.

Essay Exams

In general, essay questions are aimed at revealing your ability to make and support valid generalizations, or to apply broad principles to a series of specific instances. The question will be directed toward some major thought area. For example, in a literature course you might be asked to contrast two authors' implicit opinions about the nature of mankind. In an American History course you might be asked to discuss Madison's ideas on control of fraction, as reflected in the organization of the legislature of the United States.

Short essay questions are more apt to be aimed at your ability to produce and present accurate explanations, backed by facts. A sample short question in a literature course might be: "In a well-organized paragraph, explain Poe's theory of poetry." In a history course you might be asked to list the major provisions of a treaty, and explain briefly the significance of each provision.

Preparing for Essay Exams

1. Preparation for an essay exam, as for any exam, requires close and careful rereading and review of text and lecture notes. The emphasis in this kind of an exam is on thought areas.

2. It is often possible to find out what exam format the professor usually uses; a series of short answer types, one long essay, etc. You should ask the professor what exam format should be expected. This is not the same as asking what specific questions will be on the exam. In fact, many professors announce in advance the general areas the exam will cover—concepts, issues, controversies, theories, rival interpretations, or whatever.

3. Reviewing your lecture notes will also reveal which broad areas have been central to class discussion. Begin by asking yourself about the main concepts and relationships involved in the material you are reviewing. Review your notes with a broad view. Don't worry about detail at first. Review major headings and chapter summaries in your textbooks. Boil your material down to a tight outline form.

4. Once you have the main concepts organized in a thoughtful pattern, fill in the necessary details. On an essay exam you will be facing the task of arriving at a sound generalization and then proving it through the skillful use of detail. You must therefore have the details at your command. But remember, no detail is crucial. Select the details that best go to prove a concept.

5. Some students profit by making up sample questions and then practicing answering them. In a history course for instance you might test yourself by answering questions such as "Explain what John C. Calhoun meant by the term concurrent majority and compare his ideas to Jefferson's on majority rule."

6. Part of the groundwork for all exams is mastering the terminology used in the course. Getting this out of the way is critical.

Taking Essay Exams

1. When you first get the exam, look for the point value of each question. If the questions are not weighted equally, you need to decide how much time to spend on each question. Adjust your timing so that you allow longer time for longer answers. If necessary, borrow time from the short answers. If the point value is not listed you have a right to ask if all questions have equal value.

2. Read the directions and each question carefully. Try to understand exactly what is asked. Glance rapidly over all the questions before you start putting down your answers. An essay question always has a controlling idea expressed in one or two words. Find the key words and underline them.

3. As you skim over the test, note down key words or phrases for each question. This will serve to stimulate other ideas. Make the initial sentence of your answer the best possible one sentence answer to the entire question. Then elaborate in subsequent sentences. As ideas about other questions occur to you, immediately jot them down on scratch paper before they slip away.

4. Think through your answer before you start to write it. Use scratch paper for outlining if necessary. A little time spent on a brief outline pays big dividends for the few seconds spent. A planned answer saves you from a lot of excess words which are time consuming but worth little. If the question seems ambiguous, vague, or too broad, make clear your interpretation of the question before attempting to answer it.

5. Take care to write legibly, leave adequate margins and space your work attractively. Use good English and remember that neat papers tend to be scored higher.

6. Usually professors do not want your answer to cover everything you have learned in the course. Your essay answers should be organized, concise, to the point and with only those details needed to fill out a full picture. Do not try to reproduce the whole book. If supporting evidence is asked for, add as many details as possible.

7. Star or underline important ideas appearing late in the material. If information you have given in answer to one question ties into another, point out the interrelation. It may be worth credit.

8. Check off each question as you answer it to avoid omitting one. Re-read each answer before proceeding to the next in order to correct errors or omissions.

9. Try to budget time so that you have time to proof read your answers before you turn in the exam.

10. *Use all the time allotted to you!*

For information specific to preparing for mathematics and other technical courses, refer to the section titled "Studying for Mathematics Courses" in Chapter Three.

C H A P T E R

SIX

STRESS MANAGEMENT

CHAPTER OUTLINE

➡ Stress and Breathing

➡ Progressive Relaxation Exercise

➡ Visualizations

C hapter two began by mentioning that many midshipmen consider time to be the biggest obstacle to their academic performance. Getting organized is often the first step toward developing more effective study habits, but many midshipmen are very organized and study very effectively and still do poorly. Some students report knowing the material before the exams, but "losing it" when they sit down to take the test. This chapter will discuss this common concern and provide some practical suggestions for overcoming what has become known as test anxiety.

We know from research that when humans are faced with a stressful situation, they often tend to forget the most recently learned material and revert back to earlier learning. However, this earlier learning is frequently inadequate. This translates into poor performance and low test scores and is known as performance anxiety.

One way to deal with performance anxiety is to prepare more in advance and "over-study". That means preparing for exams well in advance and preparing for more than could possibly be on any one exam so that the earlier learning is adequate enough to enable you to do well on the test. Chapter Two: Time Management provides information that should get you started on the right path for advanced preparation.

However, for many midshipmen efficient, effective, and early study is not enough. Frequently students become so concerned about doing well that their worry actually interferes with their ability to perform. Over time and without control, stress *can* interfere with learning and performance. That is what this chapter is about.

First of all, what is stress? We use the word regularly to describe our feelings as well as the situation that seems to be causing the problem. "I am stressed out" and "The Naval Academy is really a stressful place" are common expressions. Because the dynamics of the situation are often out of our immediate control, it is more productive to focus on the feelings. The following conceptualization of the stress related to test anxiety was developed by Professor Donald Meichenbaum. His ideas provide a helpful way to look at poor performance due to stress whether the stress is due to the situation or the feelings.

Dr. Meichenbaum's work suggests that there are two components of what we call stress; a mental component and a physical component. The mental component comprises all the thoughts and worries that seem to fly through your brain as you begin to panic. For example, during a test you might look at one of the questions and start to think "Oh no, I don't know that one, I'm really blowing this test. If I don't pass this, I flunk the whole course. If I flunk, I'll be kicked out of here" and so on. The physical component consists of all the physical symptoms that go along with being stress out; headaches, upset stomach, tight muscles, etc.

Research has shown that the increasing spiral of panic can be stopped or short circuited by learning to control either the physical or the mental component. You can learn to intervene in either way to have an impact. You can learn to change how you think as well as how you act.

The first step toward change is awareness. You need to first become aware of the negative things you are saying to yourself in order to be able to change them. For most people, the outside situation is not the main problem. It is the internal reactions; the things you say to yourself that cause you to be stressed out. For example, in the preceding illustration, instead of allowing yourself to spin off on the countless negative things that can interfere with your performance you could reword what you say to yourself to be something like the following: "Oh no, I don't know that one. Well, just take it easy, maybe it will come to me later. I'll try the next one. I know I studied as much as was possible. It is now time to just take the test".

Notice that there is a factual part related to not knowing how to do the problem ("Oh no, I don't know that one"), but it is followed by a more helpful statement of self-encouragement (Well, just take it easy, maybe it will come to me later. I'll try the next one. I know I studied as much as was possible. It is now time to just take the test.").

As simple as this sounds, rewording the things you say to yourself into more positive statements can have dramatic impact on your level of confidence. And increased self confidence can help you perform without interference from irrational worry. But changing what you say to yourself, just like any behavior, takes practice. From now on, every time you catch yourself spinning off on negative, self-destructive thinking, stop, take a deep breath and reword your thoughts into more positive encouraging statements. With practice you will notice that you will be able to perform in stressful situations without undermining your own effectiveness.

As was mentioned earlier, there are two components to stress. You now have the information necessary to begin to change the effects of the mental component through changing the way you think about your own performance. You can also effect the physical component of stress by practicing a few simple exercises that will enable you to develop more self control during stressful situations. The rest of this chapter will focus on the physical part of side management.

A primary goal of stress management is to be able to perform as well as possible in a stressful situation. Because it involves performance, the goal cannot be total relaxation. You have to be active enough to perform. You cannot take a test while you are asleep, or so relaxed that you cannot get motivated. The trick is to be able to know the correct level of relaxation in order to perform to the best of your ability.

One relatively quick way to become more relaxed in stressful situations is to focus on your breathing. Most of the following material has been generously contributed by Ms. Joan McKinney who conducts a stress management workshops in the Academic Center.

STRESS AND BREATHING

Breathing has well-documented and extremely powerful effects on bodily functions. Learning to be aware of breathing is the first step toward controlling the physical and mental effects of stress. There are two basic types of breathing: diaphragm breathing and chest breathing.

The diaphragm is a large sheet of muscle, like a piece of rubber balloon stretched over the bottom of the lungs. When breathing is natural and relaxed, the diaphragm expands down on the inhale, creating a negative pressure that pulls air into the lungs. On the exhale, the diaphragm relaxes back into its original position, pushing air out of the lungs. When the diaphragm moves down on the inhale, the abdomen is naturally moved forward and expands. If you place your hand on your stomach, you will feel it bulge on the inhale, and flatten on the exhale if you are breathing diaphragmatically.

During stress there is a tendency to hold the breath, to breathe irregularly, and to exhale incompletely. When exhalation is incomplete, not enough fresh air can enter the lungs on the inhalation. This leads to a pattern of chest breathing where the diaphragm is not used. Chest or stress breathing is rapid or shallow. The chest expands and the shoulders rise with each breath since the lungs are being expanded by the small muscles between the ribs, rather than the diaphragm. This type of breathing results in poor exchange of stale air with fresh air, and blood chemistry changes that result in anxiety and fatigue. It also stimulates the sympathetic nervous system (that part of the autonomic nervous system that is especially concerned with mediating the involuntary response to alarm), producing a widespread stress response. A vicious cycle results where stress leads to chest breathing, and the physiological consequences of the shallow breathing magnify the stress response.

**NOW TAKE A MOMENT TO NOTICE YOUR BREATHING PATTERN.
WHICH IS IT?**

Learning to breathe diaphragmatically shifts physiology out of the stress mode into the relaxation mode. Begin by relaxing back against a chair, it is helpful to close your eyes. Take a deep breath and then exhale slowly and completely. Place a hand on your stomach and notice whether you can feel your stomach expand with your inhale, and flatten with your exhale. By paying attention, you will soon learn to shift automatically into diaphragmatic breathing. Heart rate will slow, blood pressure will decrease, and the sympathetic nervous system arousal as a whole will decline, leading to a subjective sense of relaxation and a decrease in anxiety and restlessness.

The following exercise will help you breath more diaphragmatically. "Deep Breathing" is adapted from *Stress Management Strategies* by Dr. Glen R. Schiraldi at the University of Maryland at College Park. Permission for adaptation of this material has been granted by Kendall/Hunt Publishing Company.

In his stress management manual, Dr. Schiraldi describes deep breathing as the "Bread and butter" of relaxation training. Deep breathing is often the first step in guided relaxation exercises such as progressive muscle relaxation and meditation. In fact, a few deep breaths can be very effective alone. This only takes a few seconds and can be extremely helpful during a stressful situation.

Deep breathing is really quite simple. Just close your eyes, and attend to the breath's naturally relaxing properties. Relax your upper body and shoulders. Take two deep breaths, filling your lungs as much as possible. As you breath in, and again as you breath out, repeat to yourself a calming word or phrase (such as "Relax", or "Calm"). With practice, this word will be associated with the feelings of being relaxed and can elicit similar feelings of relaxation. Repeat the deep breath and calming word. Then breath normally and open your eyes. Practice this exercise every time you think that you are getting "stressed out". You will begin to feel the differences almost immediately.

Another exercise called progressive relaxation is also a very helpful for training yourself to be more self controlled and relaxed.

PROGRESSIVE RELAXATION EXERCISE

Before beginning please sit up straight, with both feet on the floor, and your hands resting comfortably on the arms of the chair, or on your thighs. Once you have read and are familiar with the relaxation script, it is usually better if you can close your eyes while going through the exercise on your own.

Now, take a deep breath, inhale, exhale. Begin by allowing your feet to relax, relaxing totally and completely, relax your toes, you might wiggle them, allowing any tension to float away.

Continue breathing, relaxing more and more with each breath, allow the relaxation to continue from your feet to your legs, up the calves of your legs to your knees, to your thighs, allowing them to relax totally and completely while inhaling and exhaling.

Allow the muscles in your stomach to relax, continue that feeling of relaxation up the vertebrae of your spine, across your chest to your shoulders, down your shoulders to your arms to the very tips of your fingers. Allowing your body to relax totally and completely while you breathe in and out.

Allow the muscles in your neck to relax, the muscles in your face . . . Relax, right up to the muscles in your scalp, allow them to completely relax. Take a moment to mentally scan your body, finding any tension you may be holding on to, just let it float away, as you breathe deep, free, and even, relaxing totally and completely. Allowing your entire body to relax as you remain safe, calm, and mentally alert.

Now just allow yourself to sit there and enjoy the gentle, warm, relaxing feeling that you have developed. Try to practice this exercise as much as you can over the next week. It is something you can use in almost any situation where you are under stress and need to regroup your thoughts. You can also use this exercise to relax before going to sleep or to gain needed rest.

VISUALIZATIONS

Another technique that has become quite useful for increasing relaxation is called visualization. Once you have learned to relax with deep breathing or progressive relaxation, you can reach an even more deeply relaxed state by thinking of a special relaxation place. It can be a real place you have been, or an imaginary place you would like to go. The following visualization scripts were developed by Ms. Joan McKinney for the Academic Stress Workshops she has run at the Academic Center.

Beach Visualization

As vividly as possible, try to imagine the following scene as it is developed:

You can go to the beach. You can walk along the beach on a comfortable day watching the water as it laps up on shore, and walk along the beach feeling the warm sand beneath your feet and between your toes.

You can look out across the blue sky as the white clouds drift by and watch the sea gulls float on currents of air, drifting up and floating down, soaring in lazy circles through the air, as you breathe and relax more and more.

You can find a smooth, dry log and sit down, or stretch out on a blanket and watch the clouds drift across the sky, and the sea gulls float along on the air. You can hear their calls, you can smell the salt air, and feel the warm breeze flow across your face, as you relax comfortably and safely.

You can look out across the water and watch the waves roll in, smoothly and gently rolling to shore as you relax and enjoy the water, the sky, the beach.

Give yourself a few moments to enjoy this setting, just relax and enjoy the beach.

After several minutes bring yourself back to the present, to the room, while telling yourself you will remain physically relaxed, while being mentally alert and wide awake.

Mountain Visualization

You can go to the mountains, to a cozy log cabin in the woods. You can walk along the path to the cabin as you see a meadow of wild flowers, and rolling green, as you walk further into the woods, among the tall trees as the sunlight filters down onto the ground of leaves and earth.

You can see off to the side a small lake and look across the cool blue water, enjoying the beauty of the lake and the smell of the woods. As you continue to breathe and relax more and more, comfortably relax. Walk to the cabin and open the door and walk inside. It is cool and comfortable, a fire is lit in the fireplace and you can sit or lie down in front of the fire and relax. You can watch the flames as they play around the logs, flames of yellow and red and blue, rolling up and around the logs as you watch; safe, comfortable, and secure. You can enjoy the room and the smell of the fire in the fireplace and watch the flames and relax.

Should you choose, you can go out and sit by the lake and watch the cool blue water as it ripples across the lake and laps up against the shore. You can smell the cool clear air as a gentle breeze blows across your face, as you relax, totally and completely relax.

Now take a few minutes to enjoy this setting, just relax and enjoy the woods and the relaxed state you are in.

After several minutes bring yourself back to the present, to the room, while telling yourself that you will remain physically relaxed, while being mentally alert and wide awake.

"Special Place" Visualization

You can go to a special place, one that exists in physical reality, or one that you create and exists within your imagination. A place where you are safe, comfortable, and relaxed. A place which allows you to create, and revive your energies. You can go there now.

If you are constructing an imaginary place, what is it like, what type of place are you constructing? Is it indoors or out . . . What time of day is it, or is it evening? What type of building is it . . . Old or new . . . Modern or classical? What type of furnishings does it have? What are the colors which surround you?

Take some time to construct this special place. Spend some time there, just enjoying the surroundings, this "special place" will always be available to you when it is needed. Simply tell yourself to relax and go to this special place.

Now bring your attention back to the present, to the room, as you remain relaxed and refreshed, physically relaxed and mentally alert and confident in your abilities.

Another visualization follows that is especially valuable for students who feel that their stress interferes with their ability to perform on tests.

Test Taking Visualization

See yourself arriving for the exam a little early, getting comfortable. As you look around the room, you find you feel more and more at ease. You are in control. You breathe deeply and evenly relaxing more and more with each breath.

You studied, therefore you know the material on the exam. The information and skills needed for this exam come to you during the exam, as you deserve to do well on the test. You believe in your abilities. As you relax, you read all the directions thoroughly before beginning the exam. You make sure you understand what is being asked of you. You can do well on exams and quizzes. You have studied effectively and you remain relaxed and in control.

As the time passes and you continue through the exam, you plan your time well, allowing enough time to get to each section, with time to review and edit. You find it easy to remember information in order to complete the exam or quiz. You are relaxed and in control. You answer easy items first, when possible, building confidence, and allowing yourself to move more quickly through the test. You continue to be relaxed while remaining mentally alert.

You can take mini breaks of 5–15 seconds during the exam to refocus your efforts. You do well. You can be an expert test taker. You find it easy to remember needed information. You are comfortable. You do well on exams. You have confidence in your abilities.

Now bring your attention back to the present, to the room, as you remain relaxed and refreshed, physically relaxed and mentally alert and confident in your abilities to do well on exams.

This chapter has covered an area that is a major concern for many students. As you become more aware of the mental and physical components involved in stress, you will be able to cope with any stressful situation in which you may find yourself. With practice, you will be able to draw on any of the techniques described in this chapter in order to exert more self control. The last chapter lists many of the resources available for you at the Naval Academy. They are there for you, use them.

C H A P T E R

SEVEN

OTHER USNA RESOURCES

CHAPTER OUTLINE

➥ Academic Center

➥ Chaplain Center

➥ Chemistry Department Extra Instruction

➥ Math Lab

➥ Midshipmen Counseling

➥ Writing Center

This chapter describes academic and counseling services available to midshipmen at the Naval Academy. Under each listing is a description of the services offered, the location and phone number. These offices and individuals are here to help you. Like the techniques discussed in this manual, these resources are useful only if they are used by you. They can be of little assistance unless you ask.

ACADEMIC CENTER (X35281)

The Academic Center located in 120 Ward Hall, exists as a service unit within the Naval Academy. The Center is subdivided into four programs: Plebe Intervention, Plebe Advising, Learning Skills and Tutor Coordination. The purposes of these programs are listed below.

Plebe Intervention

The Plebe Intervention Program identifies plebes who have a high potential for encountering academic difficulties at the Naval Academy and has developed means for reducing or eliminating those difficulties. Services provided for these at-risk midshipmen include academic effectiveness classes, calculus and chemistry extra instruction and individual counseling from their assigned Academic Center adviser. Call X35281 for information about this program.

Plebe Advising

The Plebe Advising Program provides academic advice and study skills to plebes to help them adjust to the academic demands of the Naval Academy. One faculty adviser is assigned to each company during plebe summer and throughout the academic year. Plebes are assigned a permanent academic adviser when they declare a major in the spring. The plebe academic advisers are a valuable source of information and assistance. Get to know your adviser well!

Academic Counseling

Upperclass midshipmen may consult with Academic Center staff concerning their choice of major and/or other special requirements that affect their academic performance.

Learning Skills

The Learning Skills Program provides a full range of instruction to improve midshipmen learning techniques. The services provided include academic effectiveness lectures for midshipmen, and training and supervising midshipmen academic officers and company officers. Call X35281 for further information.

Tutor Coordination

The Tutor Coordination Program is available if you have worked with your course instructor, gone to EI, and still are having problems understanding course material. An Academic Center staff member can help you find an instructor who will work with you to supplement the regular classroom instruction.

CHAPLAIN CENTER (X32881)

The Chaplain Center, located in Mitscher Hall houses the offices of the academy's seven chaplains who serve and minister to the needs of the Brigade of Midshipmen. Among other things they provide personal counseling ranging from faith-centered issues through crises of life and death to future marriage plans. (Information for this paragraph was taken from United States Naval Academy Catalog.)

CHEMISTRY DEPARTMENT EXTRA INSTRUCTION (X32802)

The Chemistry Department offers scheduled "Extra Instruction" (EI) sessions in the evenings (Monday–Thursday) during both the Fall and Spring semesters. These are offered by the Chemistry Department faculty on a voluntary basis and the times and night offered are determined by the faculty members involved. The schedule for evening EI sessions for plebe chemistry can be obtained by calling the Chemistry Department.

MATH LAB (X32795)

The Mathematics Department coordinates a Math Lab during first through sixth periods on Tuesdays and Thursdays. The lab, located in Chauvenet Hall, is available to all midshipmen who need assistance with math.

MIDSHIPMEN COUNSELING (X34897)

The Midshipmen Counseling Center provides individual and group counseling to midshipmen requesting assistance in dealing with a full range of personal concerns. If you have concerns that seem to be interfering with your ability to succeed at the Academy, the Midshipmen Counseling Center can be helpful. Call X34897 to arrange for an appointment.

WRITING CENTER (X34976)

The Writing Center, located in Room G-15 Sampson Hall, provides one-on-one tutorial services to midshipmen who need or want extra writing instruction. Midshipmen may use the Writing Center by scheduling an appointment in person or by phone. The Writing Center is open for tutorials every class period Monday–Friday and after classes as scheduled.

CHAPTER

EIGHT

How To Avoid Plagiarism

Chapter Outline

- Definition and History of the Concept of Plagiarism

- Plagiarism and the Honor Concept

- Research Papers and Other Written Assignments

- Paraphrasing in Academic Writing

- Methods of Documentation

The Honor Offense for Academics

Faye Ringle Hazel, Ph.D.

Associate Professor of English

United States Coast Guard Academy

DEFINITION AND HISTORY OF THE CONCEPT OF PLAGIARISM*

Plagiarism, whether intentional or unintentional, for monetary gain or other benefit, is academia's most serious offense. At the U.S. Naval Academy, plagiarism is considered an honor offense and carries severe penalties. The *MLA [Modern Language Association] Handbook for Writers of Research Papers* provides this definition: "Plagiarism is the act of using another person's ideas or expressions in your writing without acknowledging the source . . . to plagiarize is to give the impression that you have written or thought something that you have in fact borrowed from someone else"(20). This document will expand upon this definition and will detail methods of avoiding plagiarism in research papers, homework assignments, and classroom and lab work at the Naval Academy.

The concept of plagiarism is not a modern invention; rather, it has a history nearly as long as that of the written word. The term *plagiarism*, according to the *Oxford English Dictionary [OED]*, was coined by the an-

---

*This section was previously printed and distributed as: Hazel, F.R., *Plagiarism. A Document for Teachers and Learners*. New London, CT: USCGA and appeared in *A Navigational Guide to Academic Success: The Cadet Academic Resource Manual*. New York: McGraw-Hill, Inc. adapted with permission of the author.

cient Roman poet Martial from the Latin *plagiarius,* "one who abducts the child or slave of another." Thus a *plagiarius* would be a sort of literary kidnapper. In Martial's case, his verses—his "child"—were stolen and circulated as the property of another. Such wholesale thefts form only one part of the modern academic definition of plagiarism.

During the Middle Ages, few could read, and even fewer believed that written words were the "child" or "property" of their original author. The idea that using another's words or ideas without credit might be an intellectual and moral crime reappeared only after the spread of printing in the Renaissance. In England, the term *plagiarist* did not exist until 1601, the *OED's* first reference. Ben Jonson and other Elizabethan writers believed in the importance of original thought: they distinguished between student writers, who may still learn through exact imitation of models, and professional writers, who must transcend their models. Professional writers, they believed, must always acknowledge their sources because they profit from the work.

In the last twenty years, electronic media, photographic reproduction, and the computer have added new dimensions to the old problem of plagiarism. As Michael Heim asks in a recent study, *Electric Language: A Philosophical Study of Word Processing,* "Does the conversion of twentieth-century culture to a new writing technology portend anything like the revolutionary changes brought about by the invention of the printing press and the widespread development of literacy?"(2). Despite Heim's "revolutionary changes," preventing plagiarism in academia still requires respect for intellectual property, careful scholarship and a strong personal code of honor.

Common law since the Renaissance has developed remedies for authors who, like Martial or Jonson, have been hurt financially through the loss of their works—this became known as their "copyright." There is a large body of "copyright law," which is outside the scope of this document. But common law does *not* treat the subject of plagiarism in which, though the plagiarist seems to benefit, no one else is hurt. That is exactly what happens in academic plagiarism: the only one hurt is the plagiarist, who trades long-term honor for short-term convenience or good grades.

Despite the discrepancies between copyright law and rules against academic plagiarism, today it often seems that only students suffer unusually harsh penalties for plagiarism. In advertising, business, politics and the law, plagiarists are tolerated or even rewarded. Worst of all, even professional writers may go unpunished and uncensured. Even when an author can prove deliberate plagiarism—as the late mystery writer John D. MacDonald did against Dmitri Gat in 1983 (Sherman 18)—no permanent damage is done to the plagiarist's career.

Although the writing profession does not necessarily "police itself," the academic profession certainly does. Scientists' careers have been ended by allegations of falsifying results, or even "borrowing" sources without attribution. Colleges show little mercy toward student malefactors, often voting to expel plagiarists. One such case erupted into public view when Gabrielle Napolitano took Princeton University to court in 1982. *Time* reported that she had been accused of plagiarism and judged guilty by a "ten-member faculty-student committee on discipline" (McGrath 68). Napolitano was prevented from graduating with her class; law schools which had accepted her were notified of the judgment. She lost her civil suit—and her chance at law school.

Napolitano's case is particularly interesting because it illustrates one common type of student plagiarism and two common excuses. According to *Newsweek*, she worked "as many as 37 passages lifted verbatim" into her paper from a book she had duly credited earlier (Keerdoja 17). Her excuses were time pressure—"rushing to complete her senior thesis" (McGrath 68) and ignorance of technicalities—"I didn't really realize I wasn't footnoting a lot that I really should have" (Keerdoja 17). But few college professors or disciplinary boards consider intention when assessing blame: the final written product looks the same regardless of the author's intention. In the end, writers are responsible for the work they hand in as their own. Putting one's name on an article, research paper, or homework assignment establishes the writer's intention of claiming credit for everything not specifically credited to someone else.

Even when student plagiarists are not expelled or otherwise disciplined, their guilt is a matter of permanent record. The revelation that Senator Biden had been judged guilty of plagiarism while in law school contributed to forcing him out of the 1988 Presidential race and will certainly have lasting effects on his career.

PLAGIARISM AND THE HONOR CONCEPT

Preventing academic plagiarism points to the need for strong personal codes of honor: it is too easy to rationalize that copying a math problem, or stealing a few lines from a *Newsweek* article hurts no one. Nonetheless, plagiarism runs completely counter to the very spirit of the honor concept at the Naval Academy. Plagiarism always involves lying: plagiarists necessarily lie to others about the source of their work and to themselves about having fulfilled requirements or learned the material of an assignment. Plagiarism by definition is academic cheating. Most of all, plagiarists steal ideas and the hard work of others and, thus, steal respect which they have not earned.

Avoiding plagiarism requires diligent self-inspection and the determination to learn good study habits and research methods, the same habits of mind which help internalize the honor concept.

RESEARCH PAPERS AND OTHER WRITTEN ASSIGNMENTS

It is difficult to reduce truly unconscious plagiarism—the kind we all do at some time. Beginning researchers often consider everything they read to be their own, forgetting sources overnight, wondering how their teachers can suspect such newly-minted verbal ability. Even great writers fall into this trap. Who has not felt that "naive enchantment of creation"—followed closely by chagrin over the origins of that perfect phrase, that brilliant idea? (mine was taken from Paul Valery, qtd. in Hytie 366). Here are examples of plagiarism based on bad paraphrasing or insufficient acknowledgment of source material. These examples come from an actual paper.

ORIGINAL (Tung 9)

Regional organizations have a narrower scope and are limited to certain geographical areas.

STUDENT VERSION

Regional organizations have a narrower scope and are limited to certain geographical areas.

This is plagiarism at its most blatant; though the source, Tung, is listed in the student paper's bibliography, the student has quoted verbatim ***without quotation marks or other documentation.***

> **ORIGINAL (Tung 11–12)**
>
> *The United Nations, like the League of Nations, is a juridic person even though it cannot be classified as an international government. In the opinion of the International Court of Justice, it is "a subject of international law and capable of possessing international rights and duties."*
>
> **STUDENT VERSION**
>
> *The United Nations is a juridic person even though it cannot be classified as an international government. In the opinion of the International Court of Justice, it is "a subject of international law and capable of possessing international rights and duties." (Tung 11–12)*

Here, even though the student has placed some of the quoted words within quotation marks and has even documented the source correctly, the result is *still* plagiarism because many other words are quoted **without quotation marks.**

> ### ORIGINAL (Taylor 43)
>
> **Bad omens.** *Signs of OPEC's ills came like a gusher in mid-October when Britain cut its price by $1.35 per barrel and Norway dropped its price by $1.50. Nigeria quickly followed with a $2-per-barrel drop. . . . Nigeria is just the latest member to ignore OPEC leaders' efforts to prop up prices by holding down production.*
>
> ### STUDENT VERSION
>
> *There are some bad omens within OPEC one of which is the cutting of barrel prices. In September and October of 1984, Britain cut its price by $1.35/barrel. Norway followed with a $1.50/barrel cut. Eventually Nigeria, the latest member to ignore OPEC leaders' efforts to prop up prices by holding down production, cut its prices by $2.00/barrel.*

This example breaks many rules of paraphrasing and quoting: it strings together bits of text from several different places in the original; the changes in wording are only superficial; the source is not credited.

Written assignments such as scientific reports or lab write-ups are not exempt from these rules. Documentation and paraphrasing practices, however, vary depending on the department or the subject area; students should follow the instructor's written or verbal policies.

PARAPHRASING IN ACADEMIC WRITING

Paraphrasing effectively and correctly is a difficult technique to acquire. Unfortunately for beginning writers, the definition of paraphrase varies according to the situation of the writer or speaker. Paraphrase in scholarly writing does **not** mean the same thing as paraphrase in journalism, for example. **The academic writer must give source citations for paraphrases as well as for direct quotes.**

Bad paraphrase usually results when researchers new to a field of knowledge have nothing of their own to say. They then reproduce their sources nearly unchanged, or replace the source's words with synonyms, while retaining the word order and ideas of the original. Martin and Ohmann in *The Logic and Rhetoric of Exposition* classify some paraphrasing offenses as "apt terms" and "the mosaic" (277–9). The first results when writers unknowingly reproduce short but important groups of words (such as *apt terms!*) from their sources, embedding them without quotation marks into otherwise correct summaries. The second happens when writers pick up and extend without credit metaphors borrowed from their sources.

Students all too often see research papers as "mosaics," pasting down one brightly colored tile of quotation or paraphrase after another into someone else's pattern.

Perhaps the commonest paraphrasing error is illustrated in this example from a student essay exam. The student's offense is known as "close paraphrase."

> **ORIGINAL (Thomas 311)**
>
> *The point to be made about this kind of technology . . . is that . . . when it becomes available it is relatively inexpensive and relatively easy to deliver*
>
> **STUDENT VERSION**
>
> *The main point that he uses is that his third example is the least expensive and easier to deliver than the other two.*

Notice how little the student version is changed from the original, although the writer may have thought he had "put it in his own words."

It is not possible to give an example of a really good paraphrase in this document without reprinting an entire article because a good paraphrase must reduce the material cited by many times. Here, however, is an acceptable paraphrase of the Taylor article mentioned on page 92:

> *Members of OPEC, including Great Britain, Norway and Nigeria, lowered oil prices in 1984 (Taylor 43).*

What, then, constitutes a "**good** paraphrase"? Often there is no substitute for the original words of the source. One long-time "rule of thumb" transmitted by CAPT Potter of the Coast Guard Academy is "any time you use three successive words that are not your own words, these words should be placed in quotation marks." Here, also, are some tests to apply to paraphrased material:

1. Have you reduced the original by *more than half?* That is, have you truly *summarized?*

2. Have you understood and evaluated the source for accuracy, and compared it against other sources on the same subject?

3. Have you evaluated the source's author for reliability, possible bias, and scholarly reputation?

4. Most of all, does the material you are paraphrasing serve a real purpose in your paper? Does it support a point you are making, or does it only summarize or report material already digested by someone else?

SOME INFORMATION CANNOT EVER BE PARAPHRASED.

IT MUST BE QUOTED EXACTLY AS WRITTEN.

1. Numbers—especially statistics. Changing 10% of American women to 1 out of 10 American women does not paraphrase it, nor does changing "The 13-nation cartel is the source of 15 percent" to "The thirteen nation cartel is the source of fifteen percent." Statistics, particularly, must always be documented in detail because they represent another researcher's assertions, "and may well have been superseded or challenged by other investigators" (Barnet and Bedau 87).

2. Fiction, drama or poetry. Summary of plot and theme may be possible, but paraphrase of bits of text is not. Changing to be or not to be, that is the question into Hamlet asks whether we should be or not does not illuminate Shakespeare. It is not a correct or a useful paraphrase. In addition, plot summary is rarely acceptable on college papers as a substitute for analysis.

3. Short excerpts—sentences or paragraphs. It is virtually impossible to paraphrase one sentence or paragraph at a time without using some "apt terms" (Martin and Ohmann 278) and the idea order of the source.

Instead, scholarly writers must develop quick and accurate summarizing and scanning skills: summary note-taking in some medium is usually necessary, since working directly on the word processor from sources either photocopied or electronically transmitted almost always leads to bad paraphrasing.

Note on "Common Knowledge"

Academic conventions of documentation define certain areas as "general or common knowledge," information for which writers need not cite sources. Facts found in commonly used reference books such as almanacs, dictionaries and popular encyclopedias are presumed to be free for all users. Such information as dates, places, and accepted facts (Washington's birthplace, the capital of Wisconsin, the year the Naval Academy was founded, the ballplayer who broke Babe Ruth's home run record) need not be documented, though obviously no person was born knowing these things. One way to test whether something is "common knowledge" is to check several reference sources. All will include Washington's birthplace, but only one may mention details of his education. As a general rule, document: better safe than sorry!

Avoiding Plagiarism in Homework Assignments

Much confusion arises over the difference between "collaboration," "brainstorming," and "plagiarism," especially on homework problems. Collaboration policies will vary from department to department and between instructors within a department. **However, students are responsible for ascertaining and following instructors' stated policies on this subject, as given in written or oral instructions for each course.**

All departments require students to pay special attention to crediting all sources of assistance and information—human or electronic, oral and written. Such crediting is a worthwhile habit for writers and researchers to acquire. Examples can be found on the "acknowledgments page" of any scholarly book.

On all required out-of-class assignments, at the beginning or the end of the document or (preferably) as a "content note," midshipmen **must** state any assistance they may have received on these projects. For example: on a Calculus II homework assignment, *"2/c Smart suggested using MacEquation for this derivation;"* on a paper for American Government: *"spelling was proofread by 1/c Brilliant;"* for an advanced course in the Department of Engineering: *"I used the following software to design this experiment. . . ."* In particular, midshipmen writers should be careful to indicate the degree of editorial involvement by Writing Center tutors in final papers. For example: *"LT Doe helped formulate my thesis statement;"* *"During six visits, Ms. Roe guided this paper from first to final draft."*

All statements made in this instruction also apply to electronic media, including videotapes and computer software. Users of software programs must abide by license agreements and the regulations of the Computer Services Department. Above all, the honor concept applies to copying software as surely as it does to other forms of theft of property.

METHODS OF DOCUMENTATION

Documentation of written sources has become more complicated than ever in the past ten years, as each discipline has pursued and developed standards of its own. Still, it is the responsibility of writers to find out if their potential readers—editors or teachers, especially—prefer one standard or another and to follow every convention of that standard to the letter.

The following is a summary of styles, with brief examples. Writers should always refer to the complete manual listed, rather than attempting to extrapolate correct formats from these illustrative examples.

A. "Newspaper/Magazine Style"

For informal assignments, articles, or memos, it is often desirable to place all necessary crediting within the text of the document. This is done in newspapers and in semi-scholarly magazines such as *The Atlantic* or *The New Yorker*. Exact details of publisher, place and date of publication are often omitted.

Example: A recent article in U.S. News and World Report *analyzed the woes of the OPEC cartel.*

B. "New MLA"

This is the standard, followed by English classes at the Academy, which is accepted and followed by most disciplines within the humanities. All cadets and Humanities Department instructors should have the *MLA Handbook for Writers of Research Papers* (Second Edition 1984). All English Composition texts issued within the past six years have also followed the lead of the *MLA Handbook*. This style is referred to as "parenthetical reference." This Instruction follows the New MLA style.

Example: Taylor discusses the OPEC cartel's survival problems (43).

C. APA

Another "parenthetical reference" style of documentation is that of the American Psychological Association (APA), which is followed by nearly all the social sciences. There are minor variations between older and newer editions of the *Publications Manual of the American Psychological Association*. At the Academy, all psychology courses follow this style.

Example: Taylor (1985) discusses the OPEC cartel's survival problems. It is "stuck in the trap it set for the West" (p. 43).

D. "University of Chicago"

This is the most conservative and oldest style of documentation, still followed by many journals and publishing houses. The style is explained in detail in Kate L. Turabian's *A Manual for Writers of Term Papers, Theses and Dissertations*. Chicago: U of Chicago P so it may also be referred to as "Turabian." Another standard source is *Chicago Manual of Style*. 13th ed. Chicago: U of Chicago P, 1982. This documentation style, using footnotes or endnotes, is still preferred in some government courses.

E. Other Styles

This brief listing by no means exhausts the variety of scholarly documentation systems. Here are the publication manuals of other disciplines (Gibaldi and Achtert 182):

BIOLOGY—Council of Biology Editors. Style Manual Committee. *CBE Style Manual: A Guide for Authors, Editors, and Publishers in the Biological Sciences*. 5th ed. Bethesda: Council of Biology Editors, 1983.

CHEMISTRY—American Chemical Society. *Handbook for Authors of Papers in American Chemical Society Publications*. Washington: American Chemical Soc., 1978.

LAW—*A Uniform System of Citation*. 12th ed. Cambridge, MA.: The Harvard Law Review Association, 1976.

MATHEMATICS—American Mathematical Society. *A Manual for Authors of Mathematical Papers*. 7th ed. Providence: American Mathematical Soc., 1980.

PHYSICS—American Institute of Physics. Publications Board. *Style Manual for Guidance in the Preparation of Papers*. 3rd ed. New York: American Institute of Physics, 1978.

Works Cited

A Uniform System of Citation. 12th ed. Cambridge, MA. Harvard Law Review Association, 1976.

American Chemical Society. *Handbook for Authors of Papers in American Chemical Society Publications*. Washington: American Chemical Soc., 1978.

American Institute of Physics. Publications Board. *Style Manual for Guidance in the Preparation of Papers*. 3rd ed. New York: American Institute of Physics, 1978.

American Mathematical Society. *A Manual for Authors of Mathematical Papers*. 7th ed. Providence: American Mathematical Soc., 1980.

American Psychological Association. *Publication Manual of the American Psychological Association*. 3rd ed. Washington: American Psychological Association, 1983.

Barnet, Sylvan and Hugo Bedau, eds. *Current Issues and Enduring Questions*. New York: St. Martin's Press, 1987.

Chicago Manual of Style. 13th ed. Chicago: U of Chicago Press, 1982.

Council of Biology Editors. Style Manual Committee. *CBE Style Manual: A Guide for Authors, Editors, and Publishers in the Biological Sciences*. 5th ed. Bethesda: Council of Biology Editors, 1983.

Gibaldi, Joseph and Walter S. Achtert. *MLA Handbook for Writers of Research Papers*. 2nd ed. New York: The Modern Language Association of America, 1984.

Heim, Michael. *Electric Language: A Philosophical Study of Word Processing*. New Haven: Yale UP, 1987.

Hytier, Jean. "Paul Valery et le cimetiere des reminiscences." [Paul Valery and the Cemetery Full of Reminiscences]. *Valery: New Essays in Honour of Lloyd Austin*. Ed. Malcolm Bowie, Alison Fairlie and Alison Finch. Cambridge UP, 1982. 365–383.

Keerdoja, Eileen. "Accused Plagiarist Gives Up the Law." *Newsweek* 4 Oct. 1982: 17.

McGrath, Ellie. "Questioning Campus Discipline." *Time* 31 May 1982: 68.

Martin, Harold C. and Richard Ohmann. *The Logic and Rhetoric of Exposition*. Rev. ed. New York: Holt, Rinehart, 1963.

Saalbach, Robert P. "Critical Thinking and the Problem of Plagiarism." *CCC* 21 (Feb. 1970): 45–47.

Sherman, Bob. "Author Admits Copying MacDonald." *Publishers Weekly*. 29 July 1983: 18.

Taylor, Ronald A. "For OPEC, Worst is Yet to Come." *U.S. News and World Report* 5 Nov. 1984: 43.

Thomas, Lewis. "The Technology of Medicine." *Patterns for College Writing*. Ed. Laurie Kirszner and Stephen Mandell. 2nd ed. NY: St. Martin's, 1983. 312–316.

Tung, William L. *International Organization under the United Nations System*. New York: Crowell, 1969.

Turabian, Kate L. *A Manual for Writers of Term Papers, Theses and Dissertations*. Chicago: U of Chicago P, multiple editions.

BIBLIOGRAPHY ─────────────

Flippo, Rona F. *TestWise: Strategies for Success in Taking Tests*, Belmont, Calif.: David S. Lake, 1988.

Gardner, John N., and A. Jerome Jewler. *Your College Experience: Strategies for Success*, Belmont Calif.: Wadsworth, 1992.

Gates, Jean K. *Guide to the Use of Libraries and Information Services*, 6th ed. New York: McGraw Hill, 1988.

Hyatt, C., and L. Gottlieb. *When Smart People Fail*, New York: Simon & Schuster, 1987.

Girdano, D., and George Everly. *Controlling Stress and Tension*, Prentice Hall, 1979.

Gross, Ronald. *Peak Learning*, Los Angeles: Jeremy R. Tarcher, 1991.

Lakein, Alan. *How to Get Control of Your Time and Your Life*, New York: Peter W. Wyden, Inc., 1973.

Pauk, W. *How to Study in College*, 4th ed. Boston: Houghton Mifflin, 1989.

Phillips, Anne Dye, and Peter Elias Sotiriou. *Steps to Reading Proficiency*, 3rd ed. Belmont, Calif.: Wadsworth, 1992.

Schirldi, Glenn R. *Stress Management Strategies*, Dubuque, Iowa: Kendall/Hunt, 1988.

Schmelzer, Ronald V., & Christen, William L. *Study Skills: Systems for Study*, 3rd ed. Iowa: Kendall/Hunt, 1992.

Smith, Richard Manning. *Mastering Mathematics: How to Be a Great Math Student*, Belmont, Calif.: Wadsworth, 1991.

Sotiriou, Peter Elias. *Integrating College Study Skills: Reasoning in Reading, Listening, and Writing*, 2nd ed. Belmont Calif.: Wadsworth, 1989.

Usova, George M. *Efficient Study Strategies: Skills for Successful Learning*, Pacific Grove, Calif.: Brooks/Cole, 1989.